Focus

The focus of this book is:

● to use the term 'sentence' correctly,
● to reinforce knowledge of sentences.

Tuning In

The front cover

Let's read the title together.

Look at the photographs on the front cover.

What sort of information do you think will be in the book?

The back cover

Let's read the blurb together.

What does it tell us about the book?

Contents

The contents page tells us what information is in the book, and helps us to find it. The entries are in page order, and in alphabetical order. Why do you think this might be?

Would someone like to suggest a section for us to find?

1

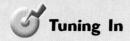

What animal is this?

What is it using its feet to do?

![eye icon] **Observe and Prompt**

Word Recognition

- Help the children with the long 'a' sound (from 'a' and silent 'e') in 'ape', if they struggle with this word.

- If the children have difficulty reading 'climb', model the blending of this word for them.

- Check the children can read the sight words on these pages with confidence (e.g. 'is', 'its', 'to').

This is an ape.
It uses its feet to climb.

2

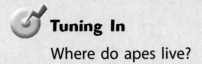

Tuning In

Where do apes live?

It holds on to the tree with its feet.

Observe and Prompt

Language Comprehension

- Check the children read with expression, taking note of the punctuation. Do they pause at a full stop?
- Ask the children what this ape uses its feet for.

3

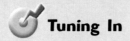

Tuning In

What animal is this?

What is it using its feet to do?

Observe and Prompt

Word Recognition

- Prompt the children to break the word 'badger' down into two syllables, before blending the whole word together.
- If the children have difficulty with the word 'uses', model the blending of this word for them.
- Help the children with the 'aw' sound in 'claws' if they have difficulty.

This is a badger.
It uses its feet to dig.

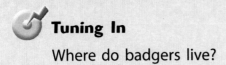

Tuning In

Where do badgers live?

It digs into the ground with its **claws**.

Language Comprehension

- Check the children are reading with good intonation, so that the sentences sound as if they make sense.
- Ask the children what sort of feet the badger has.
- Ask the children what the badger uses its claws to do.

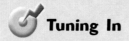 **Tuning In**

What animal is this?

What is unusual about it?

 Observe and Prompt

Word Recognition

- Prompt the children to break the word 'upside' down into two syllables, before blending the whole word together.

This is a bat.
It uses its feet to hang upside down.

6

What does it use its feet to do?

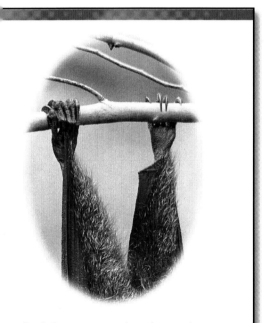

It holds on to the branch with its feet.

Observe and Prompt

Language Comprehension

- Ask the children what is unusual about the bat.

- Ask the children to look at the bat's feet. How are they different to the ape's feet?

 **Tuning In**

What bird is this?

Have you ever seen a blackbird?

What is it using its feet to do?

Observe and Prompt

Word Recognition

- Prompt the children to break the word 'blackbird' down into two syllables, before blending the whole word together.

- Help the children with the 'er' sound in 'perch' if they have difficulty with this word.

This is a blackbird.
It uses its feet to **perch**.

 **Tuning In**

Why might a blackbird perch on a branch?
(*to sing? to look for food? to rest? to look for enemies?*)

It holds on to the branch with its feet.

 Observe and Prompt

Language Comprehension

- Check the children pause at the full stops.
- Ask the children what the blackbird is using its feet to do. What does it mean to 'perch'?

 **Tuning In**

What bird is this?

What is it using its feet to do?

Observe and Prompt

Word Recognition

- If the children have difficulty reading 'eagle', model the blending of this word for them.

- Check the children are using their decoding skills to tackle the words 'catch', 'snatches' and 'talons'.

This is an eagle.
It uses its feet to catch fish.

 **Tuning In**

What do sea eagles eat?

It **snatches** fish from
the water with its **talons**.

 Observe and Prompt

Language Comprehension

- Check the children understand the term 'talons'.
- Why do the children think the eagle catches fish?

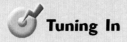 **Tuning In**

What animal is this?

What is it using its feet to do?

 Observe and Prompt

Word Recognition

- Help the children with the 'le' sound in 'turtle' if the children have difficulty with this word.

- If the children have difficulty reading 'webbed', help them with the 'ed' suffix at the end of this word.

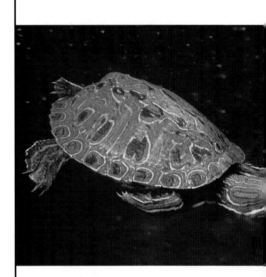

This is a turtle.
It uses its feet to swim.

Tuning In

What is special about the turtle's feet?

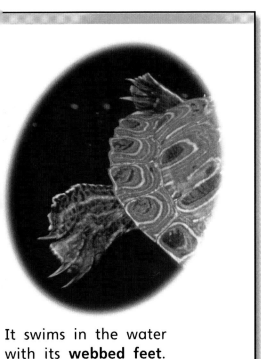

It swims in the water with its **webbed feet**.

👁 Observe and Prompt

Language Comprehension

- Ask the children what is special about the turtle's feet.
- Have any of the children ever seen a turtle?
- Do the children use their feet to help them swim?

 **Tuning In**

What is unusual about this water bird?

What is it using its feet to do?

 Observe and Prompt

Word Recognition

- Model the reading of 'walk' for the children if they have difficulty.

- If the children have difficulty reading 'lilies', model the reading of this word for them.

- Help the children with the 'oe' sound in 'toes' if they struggle with this word.

This is a **water bird**.
It uses its feet to walk.

Tuning In

What might the bird be looking for?

It walks on the **water lilies** with its long toes.

Language Comprehension

- Check the children are dividing the sentences accurately.
- Ask the children what is special about the water bird's feet.

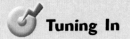

Tuning In

What do we use a glossary for?

Glossary

claws	the hard, sharp nails on animals' feet
perch	to sit or stand on something for a short time
snatches	grabs something suddenly
talons	hooked claws
water bird	a type of bird that lives near water or marshland
water lilies	a type of plant with large, flat leaves that grows in water
webbed feet	feet that have a piece of skin that joins the toes

16

 Observe and Prompt

Language Comprehension

- Check the children understand the purpose of the glossary and can use it effectively.

- Ask the children what they notice about the order of the words in the glossary.

- Check that the children realise that a word in bold signals an entry in the glossary.